Melrose Abbey

Marguerite Wood a[...]
J S Richardson

'When distant Tweed is heard to rave,
And owlet to hoot o'er the
dead man's grave,
Then go - but go alone the while -
Then view St David's ruined pile;
And home returning, soothly swear,
Was ever scene so sad and fair;'

(Sir Walter Scott, *Lay of the Last Minstrel*)

A Guided Tour

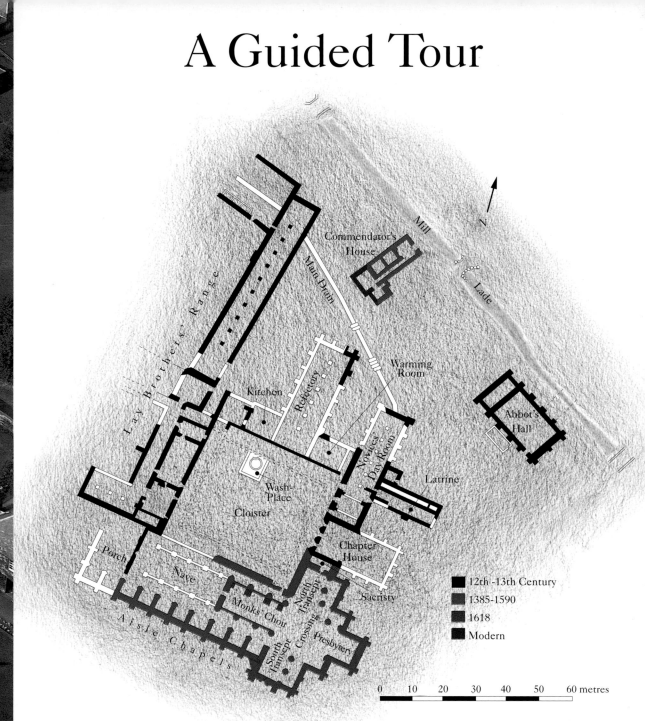

Commendator's House

Mill

N

Lay Brothers' Range

Main Drain

Warming Room

Kitchen

Refectory

Novices' Day Room

Abbot's Hall

Latrine

Wash-Place

Cloister

Chapter House

Porch

Nave

Sacristy

Monks' Choir

North Transept

Crossing

Presbytery

South Transept

Aisle Chapels

	12th -13th Century
	1385-1590
	1618
	Modern

0 10 20 30 40 50 60 metres

This tour guides the visitor around the abbey, pointing out the features of interest. It begins with the impressive abbey church, which, despite its chequered history, is the best-preserved part of the entire complex, then progresses around the cloister, visiting *en route* the Commendator's House, with its fascinating displays. Melrose Abbey served as a monastery for over four centuries, and the abbey church continued as a place of worship until 1810. During that time the place saw many changes, some brought about through changing fashion, others by the ravages of war. The visitor will see remains spanning the entire period but the building that most catches the attention is the magnificent abbey church, built from the late fourteenth to the sixteenth century following the devastation wrought by Richard II's English army in 1385.

The Abbey Church

The original church, erected in the twelfth century, was largely destroyed during the troubles of the late fourteenth century, and the structure which superceded it was of a very different architectural character.

In plan the surviving church resembled the earlier building but on a bigger scale. The transepts and presbytery were enlarged and extended further to the east and a series of chapels was built opening off the south aisle of the nave. The contemplated west end was never completed and the existing front was never entirely demolished.

The Nave

The western part of the nave was for the exclusive use of the lay brothers (see page 22) for their church services. With the disappearance of lay brothers from the order in the fifteenth century, the need to complete the nave became less urgent.

The remaining evidence for the first church (see the reconstruction on page 26) is the fragment of the **west wall** with the lower part of the entrance doorway, the foundations of the square nave piers and their connecting screen-walls, and the meagre remains of part of the north wall.

The original west front had a **porch** added on its outer, west side in the thirteenth century. There the Sunday procession was assembled. Within it are a number of burials, the fragmentary grave-covers of which still remain.

The fourth aisle chapel.

The Aisle Chapels

Eight aisle chapels survive. The three western chapels were the last to be completed, in the time of Abbot William Turnbull.

Each chapel was entered through a doorway in a wooden screen which separated the chapel from the aisle. Altars with decorative altar pieces, or retables, above stood against the east walls. The basins, or *piscinae*, in which the altar vessels were rinsed, are in the south wall. The insides of the bowls are either scalloped or

CLOISTER

PULPITUM

NAVE

NORTH AISLE

PORCH

SOUTH AISLE

?TH CENTURY ?ST WALL

AISLE CHAPEL

A monk at prayer in an aisle chapel about 1500; an artist's impression.

A basin (piscina) in one of the aisle chapels, with its beautifully carved canopy and scalloped bowl.

The vaulting over an aisle chapel.

plain and the outside ornamentation is of leaf pattern. On either side of most of the *piscinae* are niches which held the altar cruets during the Eucharist.

In the **third chapel** from the west Abbot Turnbull's initials can faintly be seen on the back wall of the *piscina*. A grave-slab against the south wall once bore a figure of a man and an inscription 'Here lies an honourable man George Haliburton [who died 1 October 1538]'.

The next **(fourth) chapel** may have been dedicated to St Michael, as his image can be seen in the central boss of the vaulting. Another boss is carved with an angel holding a shield on which are seen the decayed arms of Abbot Andrew Hunter. This chapel became the burial-place of the Pringles of Woodhouse and Whytebank, and the **fifth chapel** that of the Scotts, lairds of Gala, and the Pringles of Galashiels.

The three chapels at the east end of the nave were used as part of the post-Reformation parish kirk and the joist holes for the inserted galleries are still visible. The **sixth chapel** has a monument to David Fletcher, who was minister of Melrose before becoming Bishop of Argyll. He died in 1665.

Set into the floor of the **eighth chapel** is a thirteenth-century tomb, of prayer-desk form. The inscription on the sloping top reads 'Pray for the soul of Brother Peter, the cellarer'.

The *Pulpitum*

The massive stone screen, or *pulpitum*, set between the fourth pair of piers, separated the lay brothers' choir from the monks' choir to the east. The upper part of the screen has been destroyed, but the cornice, beautifully enriched with a stem-and-leaf pattern, remains. To the south of the central doorway is a wall-cupboard for holding furnishings used at the lay brothers' altars. Within the short passage is this ceiling boss bearing the head of Christ, and on the north side a small stair once led to the loft.

A pier in the monks' choir with its elegant lines and attractive leaf-decoration.

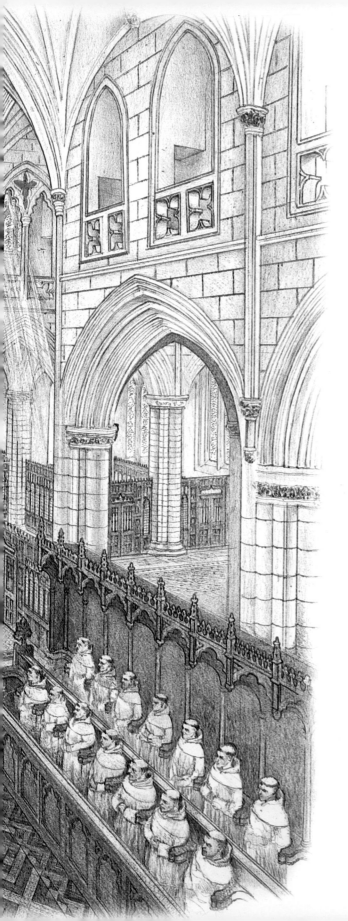

The Monks' Choir

The monks' choir occupied the space between the *pulpitum* and the crossing, and their choir-stalls were set against the stone screens which separated the choir from the aisles. The pier-caps here are beautifully arranged and carved with leaf ornament.

The monks' choir was adapted for use as a parish church in the early seventeenth century. The rib vaulting was removed and the inner arcades of the south clearstory windows were lowered and altered. Massive stone piers were built up against the north arcade to carry a plain stone vault, and walls with windows were erected at either end. The interior was fitted out with galleries. The erection of a new parish church elsewhere in the town in 1810 resulted in this kirk being abandoned and the end walls taken down, leaving the structure as it appears today, a dismal tunnel masking the beautiful proportions and designs of the fifteenth-century church.

The monks at service in their choir about 1500; an artist's impression. The present massive stone piers (below) and ugly stone vault, inserted about 1610 to form a parish kirk, utterly despoiled the splendour of this medieval creation.

The Transepts

The two transepts, or cross-arms on either side of the central crossing, housed additional altars in the eastern chapels, shut off by wooden screens, where the brethren offered up private prayers for the souls of their patrons. Each chapel had an altar under the east window. Both transepts were damaged when the central tower fell.

St Peter with key and book.

The **north transept** chapels were dedicated to St Peter and St Paul; their statues stand in canopied niches high up on the west wall of the transept. The step chapels flanking the presbytery were dedicated to St Benedict (on the north side) and possibly St Martin (on the south). The dedications of the south transept chapels are not known.

In the north-west corner of the north transept, a wide stone stair once led through the round-headed doorway to the monks' dormitory. This was the 'night-stair', used by the monks when going to and from their night services. Beside the first step is a holy-water stoup where the brethren ritually washed their hands before entering the church. In the centre of the north wall is the doorway into the sacristy, where the altar vestments and other church items were kept. High above the doorway is a long, sunken panel which was probably decorated with images of metal or wood set on the 14 large and 14 small stone pedestals. Above this are three arched openings into the clearstory passage, and over all is a circular window with its tracery still complete.

In the west wall of the **south transept** are the remains of two interesting inscriptions. (One has been removed to the Commendator's House for safe-keeping and a replica put in its place.) Both refer to a master-mason named John Morow who was born in Paris and who was probably responsible for the fine detailing of the south transept windows and for the earliest of the chapels along the south side of the nave. He was active not long after 1400.

John Morow's inscription in the south transept.

Transcribed by Reverend Adam Mylne, minister of Melrose, in the eighteenth century before they weathered, they read:

'John Morow sometimes called was I and born in Paris certainly and had in keeping all the mason work of St Andrews, the high kirk of Glasgow, Melrose and Paisley, of Nithsdale and Galloway. I pray to God and Mary both and sweet St John to keep this holy church from harm.'

and

'As the compass goes evenly about, so truth and loyalty shall do without doubt. Look to the end quoth John Morow.'

The north transept.

The presbytery from the south transept. This magnificent east end was the first part of the new church to be built following the destruction by fire in 1385 of the original building. The perpendicular window tracery hints that it may have been designed by English masons.

The Presbytery

The presbytery housed the high altar, and was lit by a magnificent 'perpendicular' window in the east wall and fine windows in the south and north walls. Under the east window are two wall-cupboards, and in the south wall there is a credence, or small table for the sacraments, and a double *piscina*. Under the side windows are recesses for tombs. Although it had originally been forbidden for laymen to be buried within Cistercian churches, the rule was relaxed and the presbytery became the burial place for the elite in society, both clerics and laymen; Bishop Bondington of Glasgow was interred beside the high altar in 1258 and Alexander II in 1249. Robert the Bruce's heart may also have been laid to rest here.

An intricate pattern of ribs and bosses adorns the vaulted ceiling over the presbytery. The central boss, positioned directly over the high altar, is a representation of the Holy Trinity attended by two angels. To the west is St Andrew holding his cross, and reading clockwise are: St Bartholemew holding the flaying knife, St Peter with the keys, St Thomas with the spear, St James the Less grasping the bludgeon, St James the Greater holding his staff and a scrip or costrel, St Paul with a sword, and St Matthias with an axe. To the south of St Andrew is a saint holding a book. Another boss has an angel and other bosses are carved with roses and leaves.

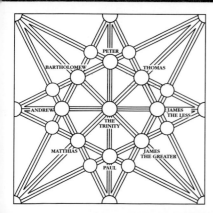

The vaulted ceiling over the presbytery, and (left) a guide to its bosses.

The Exterior of the Church

The doorway in the south transept leads to the graveyard on the south side of the abbey church. This was the final resting-place for the monks before becoming the parish burial ground. The best views of the magnificent church are to be had from there.

The exterior of the church was lavishly enriched with sculptural decoration, and although much of the statuary is missing, what has survived is still one of the most accomplished collections of medieval carving surviving in Scotland. There are gargoyles shaped like strange animals or flying dragons that belched out the roof-water, an array of demons, devils and hobgoblins on the buttresses and gables, beautiful images of Christ, the Virgin Mary, saints and martyrs in the elaborate niches, angel musicians on the projecting corbels, and heads of kings, queens, lords, ladies, monks, craftsmen and crones smirking, smiling, growling and grimacing down from their places around the windows.

Amongst the decoration on the buttresses supporting the aisle chapels is a shield bearing the royal arms of James IV, dated 1505. Under the shield is another shield which once displayed the arms of Abbot William Turnbull, and on either side a mell, or mason's mallet, and a rose – a rebus on the name Melrose. This rebus is repeated on an adjacent buttress.

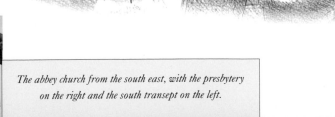

The abbey church from the south east, with the presbytery on the right and the south transept on the left.

Set in an elaborate niche adorning the westernmost high buttress is this mutilated figure of the Virgin and Child. The abbey church at Melrose, in common with all Cistercian houses, was dedicated to St Mary the Virgin, and it is appropriate that the position of this sculpture, in alignment with the *pulpitum*, marks externally the western limit of the monks' choir.

The Virgin is defaced and the Child is headless. Nonetheless, the effigy is arguably the finest piece of medieval figure-sculpture surviving in Scotland. The Virgin is veiled and crowned and the drapery of her robes falls in well-balanced folds. The infant is held on her left arm and with the right hand she holds a flower. The canopy over the Virgin and the supporting corbel are also elaborately carved.

In the niche of the next high buttress is St Andrew, now very defaced. It was not designed to fit the niche and the statue may have been brought here from elsewhere in the church.

At the wall-head of this part of the building are two charming gargoyles, or water-spouts; one depicts a winged, calf-headed beast and the other this pig playing the bagpipes!

Melrose Abbey's famous bagpipe-playing pig.

From the outside, the **south transept** forms a most attractive composition. The arrangement of the niches with their projecting canopies and carved corbels is exceptionally pleasing. The lower niche-corbels are carved with reclining figures of bearded men holding labels; the label of the figure on the west buttress is inscribed TIMET[E] DEU[M] ('Fear the Lord'), another has a scroll inscribed CU[M] VEN[IT] JES[US] SEQ[UAX?] CESSABIT [UMBRA] ('When Jesus comes the shadow will cease'), and a third displays the words PASSUS E[ST] Q[UIA] IP[S]E VOLUIT ('He suffered because He himself willed it').

The doorway is deeply recessed and at the point of the arch is a shield with the royal arms. On either side is an array of images, now headless: St Andrew, St Peter, a kneeling figure with hands clasped, a kneeling figure holding a book, St Paul and St Thomas. Set a little above in the centre of the group is a bearded man holding a scroll with the words ECCE FILIUS DEI ('Behold the Son of God'). The pedestal he supports once held a figure of Christ. Immediately above the great window is an elaborate niche which probably contained a seated figure of the Virgin. The belfry at the top of the gable was built in 1610 for the post-Reformation kirk; the Dutch bell, with its inscription IAN BURGERHVYS ME FECIT 1608 ('Ian Burgerhuys made me 1608'), still survives within it.

Corbels on the walls of the **eastern chapels** represent a monk telling his beads, angels with curly hair and smiling faces and playing musical instruments, a cook with a ladle, and a mason with his chisel and mell.

The **east gable** of the presbytery is renowned for its grace and symmetry (see the illustration on page 28). Above the window is a seated group representing the Coronation of the Virgin. On either side are statues, one on the south side being that of a mitred ecclesiastic. Quaint, cross-legged figures of men or women perch on the slopes of the buttresses.

The apex of the east gable. At the centre is the seated group representing the Coronation of the Virgin.

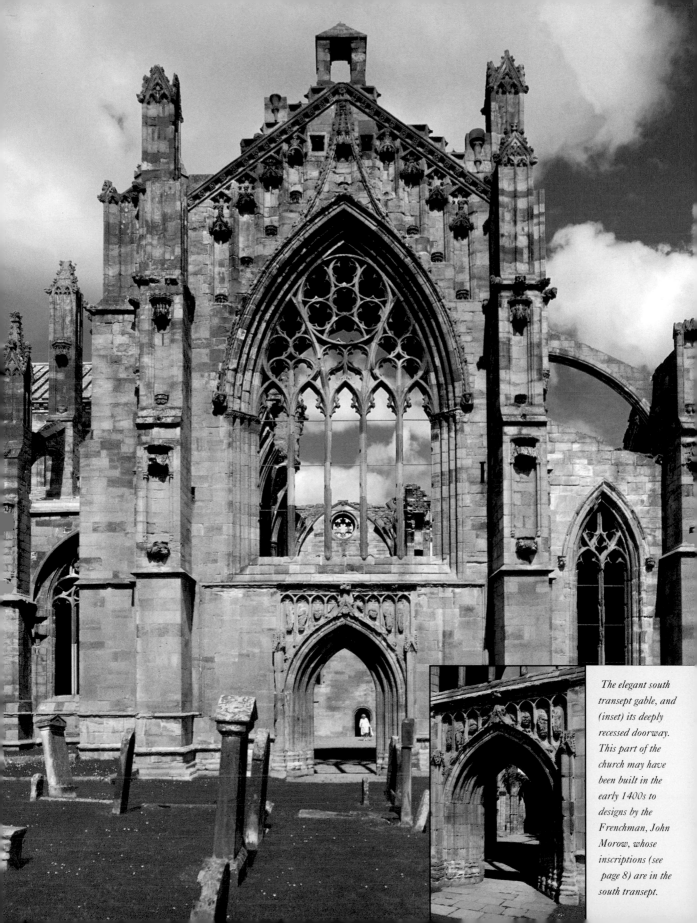

The elegant south transept gable, and (inset) its deeply recessed doorway. This part of the church may have been built in the early 1400s to designs by the Frenchman, John Morow, whose inscriptions (see page 8) are in the south transept.

The Monastery Buildings

The monks' living quarters were on the north side of the abbey church. This was unusual, the preference being to place the conventual buildings on the south side where the towering height of the church would not shut out the sunshine. The decision to build on the north was probably made so that fresh running water from the Tweed could be easily diverted for the many uses required of it.

The conventual buildings are now largely represented by low stone walls, discovered during excavations. Only the Commendator's House stands complete, albeit heavily restored. It was built in 1590 using stonework from the ruined cloister ranges. It now houses a display of objects found during excavation.

BURIAL GROUND

CHAPTER HOUSE

LATRINE

REFECTO

ABBOT'S HALL

MAIN DRAIN

COMMENDATOR'S HOUSE

MILL LADE

The east processional doorway into the church (left) and part of the elaborate wall arcades and stone benches along the south alley; painted by Robert Billings in 1832.

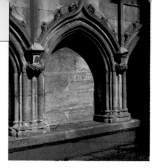

The Cloister

Except for any physical labour which required the monks to go into the outer precinct of the abbey, the Cistercian Rule insisted that they should spend their entire day within the enclosed world of the cloister. At the centre of the cloister was an open rectangular space, or **garth**, probably laid out as a garden. Around the garth were four covered **alleys**, or walks, which sheltered the monks as they passed from one building to another and where they worked. The surviving walls of the cloister, to either side of the **east processional doorway** into the church, have stone benches and elaborate wall arcades.

The East Range

The east range contained the most important rooms for the monks. Closest to their church was the **sacristy**, where much of the church equipment, vestments, altar frontals and the like, were stored, and where the priests officiating at the mass robed. Next came the **chapter house**, the main meeting room (see page 16), and beside it probably the **inner parlour**, where necessary conversation was permitted; for much of the time the brethren were sworn to silence. The end of the range was completed by a two-aisled undercroft of seven bays, probably the **novices' day room**, and to its east the lower part of the *reredorter*, or **latrine block**, serving the monks' **dormitory**, which ran the full length of the east range at first-floor level.

CLOISTER

WASH-PLACE

KITCHEN

LAY BROTHERS' RANGE

LAY BROTHERS' RANGE

Ceramic urinals of fourteenth-century date found during excavation and on display in the Commendator's House.

The Chapter House

The chapter house was the main meeting room. There the monks met every morning, to hear a chapter of the Rule, to confess misdemeanours, and to discuss business matters. It was also a favoured place of burial for abbots and other church dignitaries. Perhaps the most important interment was that of St Waltheof, the second Abbot, in 1159.

Stone coffins discovered beneath the floor of the chapter house in 1921.

In addition to ecclesiastical figures, the chapter house was the resting-place for patrons of the abbey. The *Chronicle of Melrose* records numerous interments, including Philip de Valognes, William I's chamberlain, in 1215, and a lady, Christiana Corbet, a relation of the Earl of Dunbar, in 1241; the skeleton of a woman in a stone coffin was found in 1921. Undoubtedly the most intriguing discovery in 1921 was that of a mummified heart enclosed in a cone-shaped container of lead. Decomposed iron box straps were found beside it, though nothing to indicate its history. It has been suggested that this was the heart of Robert the Bruce, interred in Melrose abbey church following its adventures on the Continent and transferred when the church was rebuilt (see page 27).

A variety of medieval pottery vessels found during excavation and on display in the Commendator's House.

The North Range

The north range housed the main domestic rooms, including the **warming room**, the only room where the monks were permitted to warm themselves, and then only for short periods each day. In the centre of the range was the **refectory**, or dining hall, where the monks ate in silence, though one of their number was delegated each day to read to them from a spiritually uplifting tome. The dining hall was originally built parallel to the north walk, but in the thirteenth century was rebuilt at right angles to it, probably to create a much larger space. The *lavatorium*, or **wash place**, was directly opposite the refectory entrance; this was a great circular basin, fed with water brought in lead pipes from a well on high ground to the south of the abbey. To the west of the refectory was the **kitchen**.

Beyond the Cloister

The *Chronicle of Melrose* for the year 1246 records that Matthew, the sixteenth Abbot, erected a magnificent hall on the bank of the stream together with many convenient offices. The foundations of his hall, the **Abbot's Hall**, are probably those just south of the mill-lade. They appear to represent a two-storey building, with a three-aisled basement, probably for storage with the Abbot's private chambers above.

The other building close to the lade is the **Commendator's House** which, when it was originally built in the fifteenth century, contained at least three rooms on the ground floor, each with a hooded fireplace. The upper rooms were entered from a timber gallery which extended along the east facade and was reached by an outside stair at the north end. The function of the building is unknown.

Three large late-medieval metal cooking vessels unearthed in the abbey many years ago and on display in the Commendator's House.

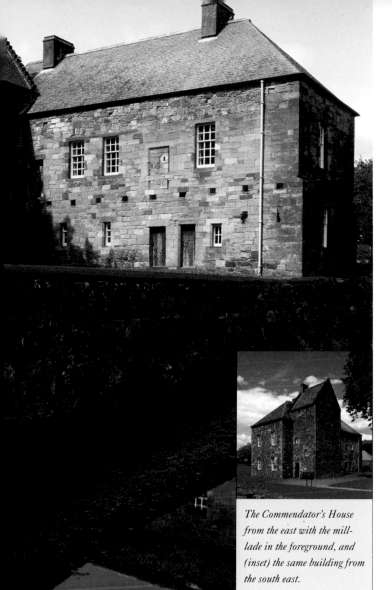

The Lay Brothers' Range

The lay brothers lived, ate and slept in their own buildings. These lay to the west of the monks' cloister. The remains of their accommodation lie to either side of the modern access road that bisects the site from west to east. The main accommodation was provided in a range that was two storeys high and extended from the west porch of the church for a distance of 108 m (320 ft). The range comprised two buildings set end to end. The north block was a continuous vaulted undercroft at ground level, 14 bays long with a central line of pillars; at a later date buttresses were added to the long walls for strengthening. Its southern end was the

The tanning pits in the lay brothers' range.

refectory. The fireplace with a tiled back in the west wall to the north indicates the position of the warming room. The remainder was cellarage, and all the spaces were originally divided by wooden screens, later replaced by crude stone walls at the second, fourth and twelfth bays. The building which ran at right angles from the north end of it housed the latrines and three pits, probably used for leather-tanning.

The Commendator's House from the east with the mill-lade in the foreground, and (inset) the same building from the south east.

In 1590 it was converted into a private house for James Douglas, the last Commendator of the abbey. The gallery was removed and a square stair-tower furnished with gun-holes was added at the south-east corner. Vaulted cellars and a kitchen were inserted in the ground floor and the upper floors reorganised.

To the north of the Commendator's House is the **mill-lade**; it is fed by a cauld or dam across the Tweed some 460 m (1/4 mile) to the west of the abbey. Part of its function was to power the abbey's mills, but before it reached the westernmost abbey buildings, part of it was diverted and carried along a **main drain**, or sewer, to flush the latrines in the east range.

The south block may have started as the refectory, and later been converted into a wash-place or workshop. The upper storey was the dormitory, and from it a night-stair led down into the north-west corner of the church.

The main drain.

'Melrose Abbey'; painted by James Ward.
(COURTESY OF THE NATIONAL GALLERIES OF SCOTLAND.)

The Story of the Abbey

Melrose Abbey is arguably the finest of the Scottish Border abbeys and its story is a fascinating one. It begins deep in the Dark Ages with the arrival of Celtic monks to Old Melrose just 2.5 miles (4 km) to the east of the present abbey, continues with the advent of the Cistercians in 1136, who through their diligence and hard work created one of the richest and most magnificent abbeys in Scotland, and ends not at the Reformation in 1560 but in the early nineteenth century with the building of a new parish kirk elsewhere in the prosperous town of Melrose.

Melrose Abbey has close associations with many famous historical figures, among them St Aidan, St Cuthbert and St Waltheof, King David I and King Robert the Bruce of Scotland, and King Richard II of England.

Old Melrose

The lid of St Cuthbert's coffin, carved with the figure of Christ. (COURTESY OF THE DEAN AND CHAPTER OF DURHAM CATHEDRAL.)

'Now he [St Cuthbert] entered first the monastery of Melrose which is enclosed for the most part by a loop of the river Tweed, and which was then ruled by its abbot, Eata, the most meek and simple of all men.'

The Venerable Bede, in his
Life of Saint Cuthbert

A little to the east of Melrose, beside the winding River Tweed, is a secluded spot called Old Melrose. It is here that Melrose's story truly begins shortly before the year 650. It was at this time that St Aidan of Lindisfarne established a monastery here, 'Mailros', bringing monks from the Columban monastery on Iona. Mailros then lay within the Anglian kingdom of Northumbria, and its first Abbot, Eata, was one of 12 Saxon youths taught by Aidan. The first Prior, St Boisil, a quiet and unassuming monk, gave his name to the local village of St Boswells, and another monk, St Bothan, is remembered in the nearby village of Bowden.

Old Melrose's most famous son was St Cuthbert. A Borderer by birth, Cuthbert entered the monastery following a vision whilst shepherding on the Lammermuir Hills, apparently on the very night St Aidan died in 651. The young lad, who loved games and pranks, in time succeeded Boisil as Prior of Old Melrose and in 664 became Prior of Lindisfarne. Whether he returned to the place of his youth is not known, but his body was returned two centuries later, for safe-keeping during the Danish raids on Lindisfarne. By this date Old Melrose was no more. The abbey that Cuthbert knew had been destroyed in 839 by Kenneth MacAlpin, King of the Scots of Dalriada. But the sanctity of the place lived on, and between 1073-5 it served as a retreat for Prior Turgot of Durham, later confessor and chronicler to St Margaret of Scotland.

Little is known of the planning of these early monasteries, but at Old Melrose at least the boundary is visible, a *vallum* or ditch cutting off the neck of the promontory on which the monastery stood. At the heart of the monastery was the church and around it the individual cells or huts of the monks, their granaries, storehouses, workshops and guestrooms.

*The site of Old Melrose lies in the foreground, within
a winding of the River Tweed. In the distance are the
three peaks of the Eildon Hills (Trimontium) and to
their right the town of Melrose with its abbey. The photograph
was taken from Scott's View, near Dryburgh Abbey, a
favourite haunt of the noted antiquarian and novelist.*

When St Margaret's youngest son, David I,
invited the Cistercian monks from Rievaulx to
set up their first house in Scotland, he chose
Old Melrose. The monks seem not to have
found the site to their liking and opted for a spot
a little further west called Little Fordell, now
Melrose itself. A church of sorts, however, did
continue at Old Melrose for at least another
century.

The Cistercians

A Cistercian or 'white' monk.

'Our food is scanty, our garments rough; our drink is from the stream and our sleep is often upon our book. Under our tired limbs there is but a hard mat; when sleep is sweetest we must rise at bell's bidding...Self will has no place; there is no moment for idleness or dissipation...Everywhere peace, everywhere serenity and a marvellous freedom from the tumult of the world.'

Aelred, Abbot of Rievaulx (1147-67)

The Cistercian movement was established in 1098 at Cistercium (modern Citeaux, near Dijon) by monks from the Cluniac house at Molesme. It was one of numerous attempts to return a degenerate monastic system to the strict Rule of St Benedict. The rise of the order was meteoric despite its uncompromising insistence on poverty and labour. The first Cistercian house founded in Britain was Waverley, in Surrey, in 1128. Rievaulx followed three years later. Melrose, in 1136, and Dundrennan, in Galloway, in 1142, were both established from there. Nine more Scottish Cistercian houses followed; the last, Sweetheart, in Galloway, as late as 1273.

The order soon developed an intensive agricultural system. Its monasteries were set up in remote places, 'far from the concourse of men'; its lands and industries were worked solely by and for the community. The order achieved this by admitting lay brothers into its ranks, men who took the monastic vows and lived a cloistered life but who undertook a greater part of the manual labour at the expense of the religious life. They were permitted longer sleep and more food for their pains.

A Cistercian lay brother chops down a tree and with it a colleague! (COURTESY OF THE BIBLIOTHEQUE MUNICIPALE, DIJON.)

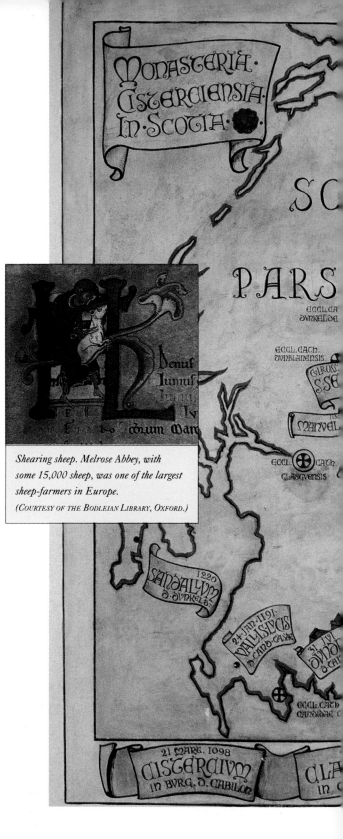

Shearing sheep. Melrose Abbey, with some 15,000 sheep, was one of the largest sheep-farmers in Europe. (COURTESY OF THE BODLEIAN LIBRARY, OXFORD.)

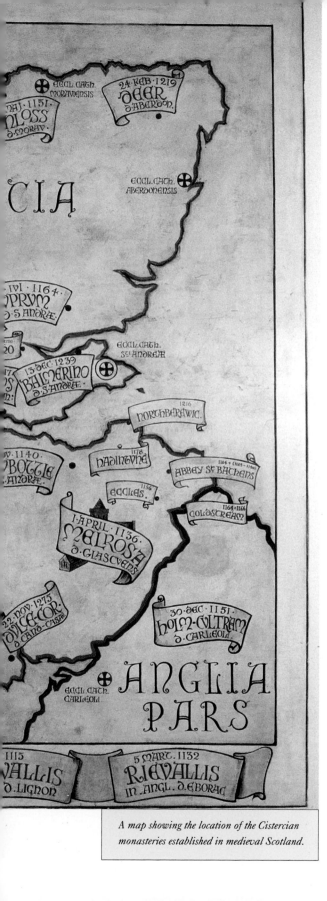

A map showing the location of the Cistercian monasteries established in medieval Scotland.

The monks and lay brothers wore undyed or white woollen habits and became commonly known as 'the white monks'. Beneath their habits they wore no undershirts or woollen breeches – not even in Scotland! Their diet was strictly vegetarian, but wholesome.

Bishop Gerald of Wales wrote: 'Give the Cistercians a wilderness or forest, and in a few years you will find a dignified abbey in the midst of smiling plenty'. In this was the great contradiction of the Cistercians; although dedicated to poverty they contrived to create unprecedented wealth. The order was anti-intellectual and yet it attracted some of the best-educated men in Europe, who found expression in revolutionising agriculture and architecture.

The life of a Cistercian was dedicated to prayer and physical work. His day, like the buildings he occupied, was laid out by the constitution of the order, and regulated from Citeaux. Daily life revolved around the eight set 'hours' or church offices; the remainder of the monk's day was divided by work, sleep or private prayer. The abbot at his head was assisted by other officers who supervised the various activities. These included the prior, his deputy, the precentor, who arranged the church services, the sacrist, who was responsible for furnishing

A cellarer takes a sneaky swig from the barrel. (COURTESY OF THE BRITISH LIBRARY.)

the church, the cellarer, who provisioned the cellars, the novice master, who instructed new recruits, and the almoner, who looked after the poor. Links with the outside world were restricted to the abbot, who was frequently absent on State business, the cellarer, and the lay brethren, who staffed the granges, or farms.

King David I and the Founding of the Abbey

'The abbey of St Mary of Melrose was founded on Monday, being the second day of Easter week [23 March] and its first abbot was Richard.'

An entry in the *Chronicle of Melrose*

King David I, from a charter of 1159 granted to Kelso Abbey.
(*Courtesy of the Duke of Roxburghe.*)

The foundation of Melrose Abbey in 1136 was part of King David's major reorganisation of the Scottish Church. During his years in power, David was responsible for the foundation of 15 major religious houses. These included the Border abbeys of Kelso, Jedburgh and Melrose; Dryburgh was founded by David's Constable, Hugh de Moreville.

King David invited the Cistercians from Rievaulx Abbey, in Yorkshire, to build a house at Melrose, and he ensured the prosperity of the new monastery by liberally endowing it with land and other assets. He also encouraged others to become benefactors, and in this way the monks received endowments of land as far away as Carrick, property in towns like Berwick, then Scotland's chief port, and Edinburgh, as well as other assets like fishing rights, salt-marshes and a peat-moss. Such was the popularity of Melrose that it became one of Scotland's wealthiest medieval monasteries. It was also held in great affection. Robert Avenel, Lord of Eskdale, and Richard de Moreville, High Constable of Scotland, both major patrons, enrolled as novices there in the evening of their days, and Alexander II, on his death-bed in far-off Kerrera, near Oban, in 1249, gave strict instruction that his body be laid to rest in its abbey church.

The Lammermuir Hills, the upland area to the north of Melrose where St Cuthbert was a shepherd-boy in the seventh century and where much of the medieval abbey's wealth was created on its sheep farms, or granges. The ruins of Penshiel Grange are circled.

A monk works on the Chronicle of Melrose (a costume figure by Anne Carrick) and (right) an ink-pot unearthed at the abbey; both are on display in the Commendator's House. The Chronicle, recording national events as well as events in the life of the monastery, was produced by a succession of monks from the time of the abbey's foundation until the late thirteenth century.

St Waltheof, a step-son of David I and the second Abbot of Melrose, was buried in the chapter house. He was renowned for performing miracles. Eleven years later his tomb was opened by Ingelram, Bishop of Glasgow, and his body found in a perfect state. Again in 1206, when a mason called Robert was working on a new tomb cover, he peeped inside and found the body still complete. By 1240, however, when a few small bones were removed for relics, the saint was found to have decomposed. In 1921, excavations in the chapter house uncovered three stone coffins close to the doorway; could one be St Waltheof's tomb? Three fragments of a monumental tomb, finely dressed and moulded and still bearing traces of gilding with gold leaf, were recovered. They possibly formed part of the saint's shrine, and are now on display in the Commendator's House.

Rievaulx Abbey, Yorkshire, the mother house of Melrose.
(COURTESY OF ENGLISH HERITAGE.)

A thirteenth-century tomb-stone found in the abbey and on display in the Commendator's House.

The First Church

'The church of St Mary, Malros, was dedicated upon the fifth of the kalends of June [28 June] being Sunday.'

An entry in the *Chronicle of Melrose* for the year 1146

The 13 monks arriving from Rievaulx (Abbot Richard and 12 others, signifying Christ and his disciples) began the building of their new abbey in strict accordance with the Rule of the order, constructing temporary accommodation first before embarking on the east end of the abbey church. The work must have been sufficiently advanced by 1146 to enable the dedication service to take place. But it should be remembered that the work of erecting the monastery could take 50 years and more, particularly as the domestic buildings had to be progressed along with it.

Little of this first church is now visible, but excavations have identified the main elements of the plan. It follows closely the original plan of Rievaulx, which in its turn was probably modelled on that at Clairvaux, another Cistercian house in eastern France, the monastery from which Rievaulx was founded. The church had a rectangular presbytery two bays long. The presbytery was flanked by two single-bay chapels and two transepts, or cross-arms. Together they formed an unusual stepped arrangement at the east end. Beyond the crossing, the aisled nave stretched back for a further nine bays. The west door was centrally placed and beyond it a porch was built later.

The influence of the monks' Yorkshire origins can be seen in the architecture. A stepped east end within a Cistercian house is rare in France and the only other British example is at Fountains Abbey. The arrangement of the nave at Melrose closely echoed that at the mother house of Rievaulx. The simplicity of the architecture for which the Cistercians were renowned at this date is evident in the surviving west wall.

Prayer was central to the lives of the monks, and the church provided the focus of that work. The services were frequent and the architecture was adapted to reflect the liturgical and processional needs of the community.

The presbytery at the east end housed the high altar, while lesser altars in the transept chapels permitted the ordained monks to say private masses, partly for the souls of those who had patronised the abbey with endowments. 'May their happy alms ever be in eternal memory', records the *Chronicle* in 1188, alluding to the generosity of the de Moreville family.

The monks' choir occupied the area within the crossing and into the eastern part of the nave. The lay brothers' choir, with its own altar, took up the remainder of the nave, and the two choirs were separated by a screen, called a *pulpitum*. A stair connected the north transept with the monks' dormitory, to allow them to attend night services without having to brave the outside cold; hence its name the 'night-stair'. There was a similar provision in the north-west corner of the nave for the lay brethren.

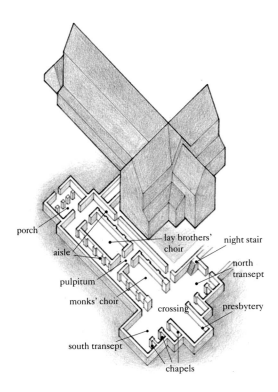

porch
aisle
pulpitum
monks' choir
south transept
chapels
lay brothers' choir
night stair
north transept
crossing
presbytery

The arrangement of the first church.

The abbey church from the west. The low wall in the foreground was the west wall of the first church, and is the only part of that building surviving today.

War with England

'...in the same monastery...one monk who was then sick and two blind lay brethren were killed in the dormitory by the English, and a great many more were wounded unto death. The Lord's Body was cast forth upon the High Altar and the pyx wherein it was kept taken away.'

An entry in the *Chronicle of Melrose* recording the sack of Melrose by the army of Edward II of England in 1322

The first 200 years passed peacefully enough, the only disruptions to the monastic routine being those imposed by the construction works and numerous land disputes. But this tranquil idyll was suddenly disrupted in 1296 with Edward I of England's invasion, and Melrose, at the heart of the Border country, was to suffer repeated depredations at the hands of the 'auld enemy' for the next 250 years.

In 1322 Edward II's army sacked Melrose and King Robert the Bruce (1306-29) helped the monks to rebuild their abbey. This devotion to the Cistercians at Melrose received final recognition when, a month before he died, Bruce instructed that his heart be buried within the abbey. Other chroniclers, however, tell how, on his deathbed, he made his close friend, 'the Good' Sir James of Douglas, swear to carry his heart against the enemies of Christ, how Sir James fell fighting against the Moors in Spain, and how, finally, the heart was brought back to Scotland by Sir William Keith and interred within the abbey. The great King's body had already been laid to rest in Dunfermline Abbey.

The skull of King Robert the Bruce; a plaster cast made by William Scoular in 1819 shortly after the discovery of the great king's body at Dunfermline Abbey (COURTESY OF THE NATIONAL GALLERIES OF SCOTLAND), and (right) a costumed figure by Anne Carrick on display in the Commendator's House portraying Sir William Keith bearing King Robert's heart to Melrose.

A Phoenix from the Ashes – the Later Church

In 1357, David II, Robert the Bruce's son, returned from long imprisonment in England; an uneasy peace returned to the Border country whilst the English monarchy was now more preoccupied with the situation in France. In 1385, the 'auld alliance' between Scotland and France led to the Scots army invading England, an attempt to divert England's attention away from the Continent by rattling their back gate. The raid brought devastating results for Scotland in general and the Border in particular. Richard II's army invaded in strength and burned and pillaged its way through the eastern Border country. They destroyed everything, bemoaned the chronicler, 'saving nothing and burning down with the fiery flames God's temples and holy places, to wit the monasteries of Melrose, Dryburgh and Newbattle'.

The monks looked at their smoking ruin and decided there was nothing for it but to rebuild anew. Over the course of the next 100 years and more, the masons set about creating what is still one of the marvels of medieval church architecture anywhere in the British Isles. The quality of their craftsmanship is quite superb; the richness of the ornamentation awe-inspiring – in stark contrast with the plain lines and unadorned surfaces of its burned-down predecessor. The Cistercians had moved a long way from the simple aspirations of their founding fathers.

The magnificent presbytery and flanking transepts (above), and the elegant south transept (right); painted by Robert Billings in 1832.

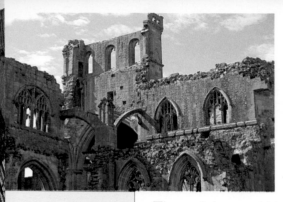

The presbytery and north transept with the central crossing tower behind. Building work began at this east end, probably with English masons, and included the great east window and presbytery vaulting (left).

The work began within a year or two of the burning, probably under the aegis of Richard II who seems to have regarded southern Scotland as having been conquered. He certainly made financial provision for the work in 1389, and the architectural evidence supports the belief that part at least of 'the new werke of thaine kirke of Melros' was carried out by English masons. The clue is in the windows of the new presbytery, where the tracery is mostly in the English 'perpendicular' style; their nearest parallels are in eastern England, as at Beverley St Mary in Yorkshire. That responsibility for the building work passed after a while to masons from another tradition is also evident in the fabric for there is a distinct change in style, most obviously in the south transept and the side chapels in the nave. Here the more flowing window tracery has been inspired by European buildings, and two inscriptions in the south transept record that this particular part of the work was supervised by a French-born master-mason, John Morow.

A detail of the tracery in the south transept window and (left) the octagonal crocketed spire of the south transept stair. The more flowing window tracery in the south transept and in the south aisle chapels (far right) suggests that by the time building work reached here the original English masons had been replaced by others influenced by French fashion.

The rebuilding work continued through the fifteenth and into the sixteenth century; James IV distributed drink-silver to the masons during his visits in 1502 and 1504. It is likely that the church was never actually completed, but even in its unfinished state it must have been magnificent to behold, both inside and out. Today's visitor has only the splendour of the masonry to admire, with its exquisite, captivating and humorous carvings. The pretty rose-tinted sandstone was quarried from the neighbouring Eildon Hills. The glazed floor tiles, coloured yellow, green or brown and set in geometric patterns, can be seen on display in the Commendator's House. Alas, of the monks' choir stalls, ordered from Cornelius de Aeltre of Bruges, nothing at all remains.

Decline and
Fall

'The monks of Melrose made gude kail
On Fridays when they fasted;
Nor wanted they gude beef and ale,
As lang's their neighbour's lasted.'

From an old Border ballad hinting at
the relaxed nature of monastic life at the time
of the Reformation.

*Abbot Hunter's Tower,
at Mauchline, Ayrshire;
an early engraving. This
pleasing little tower house
provided a comfortable
lodging for the Abbot on his
occasional visits to the
abbey's Carrick estates.*

Little is known of the day-to-day story of
Melrose as the Middle Ages wore on, but
what is clear is that it was not only the church
architecture that was changing. The economy
continued to revolve around the sale of
high-quality wool, but was now produced on
tenanted farms rather than on granges run by
the lay brothers, who had probably disappeared
by 1443 when their former choir in the nave was
adapted for parish worship. The Abbots were
also taking on roles different to those expected
of them by their founder. Now, as statesmen
and courtiers, they were frequently absent
from the cloister, leaving control of the
monastery to their Priors. Abbot Andrew Hunter,
for example, was the King's Treasurer in 1450.

The dilution of the strict Cistercian Rule, even
for the monks, is evident in a ruling made by
the Abbots of Coupar Angus and Glenluce
who decreed in 1534 that the practice at
Melrose of allowing individual monks to have
private lodgings and gardens must cease on
pain of excommunication. A dispensation was
permitted for the gardens to continue as long
as the produce was for the good of the whole
community.

One sign of the decline was the appointment
in 1541 of James V's eldest son, James Stewart,
as Commendator, or administrator of the
monastery and the enforced resignation of the
last Abbot, Andrew Durie. The new incumbent
was an infant at the time!

*The monastery precinct about 1500;
an impression by Alan Sorrell.
The coats-of-arms are those of
Abbots Andrew Hunter, William
Turnbull and Andrew Durie.*

The End of an Era

'...without the kirk be repairit this instant sommer God service will ceise this winter'.

A complaint lodged by the sub-prior and three monks against the Commendator in 1556

By the time of Abbot Durie's resignation the abbey was already experiencing the effects of Border warfare again. In 1496 James IV had used the monastery as his headquarters during his raid into Northumberland. In 1502 he received the English ambassador there and in 1528 the monks were called on to provide food for the army of Regent Albany and 'to remane in thair abbayis substantiouslie accumpaneit and weill bodin in feir of war for defence of the realme'.

Abbot Durie got away just in time to avoid the full horrors of war. The death of James V in 1542 and the accession of James Stewart's half-sister, Mary, to the throne led to the 'War of the Rough Wooing'. In 1544 the English set fire to the town, pillaging and desecrating the abbey church and its tombs. In the following year they repeated the action, but the English commander, Sir Ralph Evers, was killed soon after at the battle of Ancrum Moor; ironically his body was buried in the very church he himself had looted.

By now the will was gone to repair the devastated fabric. The few remaining monks protested to their Commendator, in vain. They bemoaned the fact that 'the conventuale observance and ordinar ar not keipit', but still nothing was done to restore 'the kirk and dourtor [dormitory] and uthur placis quhair maist neid is'. By 1556 they warned that 'without the kirk be repairit this instant sommer God service will ceise this winter'. Four years later came the Reformation, and the requirement for their form of 'God service' was at an end.

The church by floodlight.

'If thou would'st view fair Melrose aright,
Go visit it by pale moonlight;
For the gay beams of lightsome day
Gild, but to flount the ruins grey.'

(Sir Walter Scott,
Lay of the Last Minstrel)

Just how many monks were in residence in 1560 is not known; in 1539 the number was down to 22, including the Abbot and Prior. Desirous of retaining their 'private pensions', they renounced monasticism and embraced the reformed religion. But the buildings were falling down about their ears. In 1573 Sir Walter Scott of Branxholm was accused by them of dismantling 'the inner queir' [the monks' choir], the 'uter kirk' [the nave], 'the stepile and croce kirk of the same' [the tower and transepts] and carrying off the stones, timber, lead, iron and glass and later of taking away similar materials from the abbot's hall. His excuse? He was only removing the materials to save them from falling into the hands of the English!

Soon after 1590, Dan Jo Watson, who had shortly before signed himself as 'only convent', passed away. The story of almost 1000 years of monasticism at Melrose died with him.

Dan Jo Watson's death was not quite the end of the story though. The crumbling abbey church continued to be used by the townsfolk and about 1610 part of the former monks' choir was converted for parochial use and a belfry was erected at the top of the south transept gable.

The inscribed lintel over the entrance into the Commendator's House.

Already by this date part of the ruined cloister had been retained by the last Commendator, James Douglas, and converted into an acceptable residence. When that headstrong nobleman was executed, the abbey lands were sold by the Crown in small lots to various nobles. The lordship of Melrose went to the Earls of Haddington, and from them it was bought by Anne, Duchess of Buccleuch, widow of the ill-fated Monmouth. With the erection in 1810 of a new parish kirk on the Weirhill, elsewhere in the town, the story of Melrose Abbey finally came to a close.

A communion token from the old parish kirk, on display in the Commendator's House.

FURTHER READING

On Melrose Abbey:

The Royal Commission on the
Ancient and Historical Monuments
of Scotland,
Inventory of Roxburghshire II (1956).

On abbeys generally:

J Bilson
'The architecture of the Cistercians'
Archaeological Journal 56 (1909).
P Fergusson
The Architecture of Solitude (1984)
R Fawcett
Scottish Abbeys and Priories (1993)
D Robinson (ed.)
The Cistercian Abbeys of Britain (1998)

'The Town of Melrose'; painted by I Clark in 1825.
The new parish church, built on the Weirhill in 1810,
is visible just to the right of the ancient abbey.